Analyzing the News

Introduction

The Bible was written to, for, and by real people. All the words of the Bible were written to real people living at the time the words were written. All the words of the Bible were written for real people, whenever they might live. All the words of the Bible were written by real people. What to write and how to write it was told to the writers by the Holy Spirit of God. Peter wrote (2 Peter 1:21), "...holy men of God spake as they were moved by the Holy Ghost." Nevertheless, real people were both the instruments of the writing and the reason for the writing.

Because God wanted real people—people He loves—to understand His will and walk in His way, He caused many of His teachings to be told in story form. Even history is a kind of story. Another means God used was poetic form. Poetry speaks to the feelings of people.

In this LIFEPAC® you will study the literary forms that are found in the Bible. You will study how to make a good written report, and you will make a written report on a Bible theme.

Objectives

Read these objectives. The objectives tell you what you should be able to do when you have successfully completed this LIFEPAC. Each section will list according to the numbers below what objectives will be met in that section. When you have finished this LIFEPAC, you should be able to:

1. Identify seven Bible literary forms.

2. Describe the main characteristics of Bible stories and parables.

3. Choose a specific topic for a written report.

4. Identify sources of information for a written report.

5. Describe the main characteristics of Hebrew poetry.

6. Describe the main characteristics of Hebrew prophecy.

7. Take notes for a written report.

8. Identify the purpose of writing a report.

9. Outline notes for a written report.

10. Tell why Bible history is different from other history.

11. Tell what is meant by the term "The Law" as used to identify Bible writing.

12. Draft, correct, and finalize a written report.

13. Spell new words correctly.

14. Correctly form letters.

Survey the LIFEPAC. Ask yourself some questions about this study and write your questions here.

_____
_____
_____
_____
_____
_____
_____
_____
_____
_____
_____
_____
_____
_____
_____
_____
_____
_____
_____
_____

LANGUAGE ARTS 609
Reading the Bible

LIFEPAC Test is located in the center of the booklet. Please remove before starting the unit.

Authors:

Elizabeth Loeks Bouman

Sandra Stone, M.A.

Editor:

Richard W. Wheeler, M.A.Ed.

Consulting Editor:

Rudolph Moore, Ph.D.

Revision Editor:

Alan Christopherson, M.S.

MEDIA CREDITS:

Page 7: © Patrick Poendl, iStock, Thinkstock; **8:** © Lit Liu, iStock, Thinkstock; **13:** © maurusone, iStock, Thinkstock; **26:** © Lenar Musin, iStock, Thinkstock; **31:** © Heatherfaye, iStock, Thinkstock; **33:** © OkoSwanOmurphy, iStock, Thinkstock; © Plisman, iStock, Thinkstock; **48:** © allanswart, iStock, Thinkstock; **50:** © Szepy, iStock, Thinkstock.

Alpha Omega
PUBLICATIONS

804 N. 2nd Ave. E.
Rock Rapids, IA 51246-1759

1. SECTION ONE

Did you know that most of the "Bible stories" you have enjoyed hearing in Sunday school are "short stories" just like the ones in literature? You will study the short-story form and learn to find the short stories in the Bible. You will also learn about parables in the Old Testament as well as the New Testament. You will learn the way to start to make a report and begin the preparations for making a report on a Bible topic. You will also learn to spell new words with two, three, and four syllables. In handwriting you will practice writing difficult letters.

Section Objectives

Review these objectives. When you have completed this section, you should be able to:

1. Identify seven Bible literary forms.
2. Describe the main characteristics of Bible stories and parables.
3. Choose a specific topic for a written report.
4. Identify sources of information for a written report.
13. Spell new words correctly.
14. Correctly form letters.

Vocabulary

Study these words to enhance your learning success in this section.

delegation (del' u gā' shun). A group of representatives.

exploit (eks' ploit). Bold unusual act; daring deed.

intensify (in ten' si f ī). To make stronger in feeling or idea.

mock (mok). Laugh at; make fun of.

parallelism (par' u lel iz um). Likeness; correspondence; agreement.

raid (rād). An attack.

specific (spi sif' ik). Definite; precise; particular.

stimulate (stim' yü lāt). Excite; rouse to action.

unleavened (un lev' und). Not leavened; made without yeast.

valour (*also* **valor**) (val' ur). Bravery; courage.

Note: *All vocabulary words in this LIFEPAC appear in* **boldface** *print the first time they are used. If you are unsure of the meaning when you are reading, study the definitions given.*

Pronunciation Key: hat, āge, cãre, fär; let, ēqual, tėrm; it, īce; hot, ōpen, ôrder; oil; out; cup, pu̇t, rüle; child; long; thin; /ŦH/ for **th**en; /zh/ for mea**s**ure; /u/ or /ə/ represents /a/ in **a**bout, /e/ in tak**e**n, /i/ in penc**i**l, /o/ in lem**o**n, and /u/ in circ**u**s.

BIBLE STORIES, PARABLES, AND PROVERBS

Stories are good teachers. Stories are more interesting than plain teaching, and stories show the right way by examples. Even short illustrations are stories of a kind. The "short story," however, is a recognized literary form. Short stories, as a recognizable literary form, are found in the Bible. Parables are stories, too, but have a different form. Proverbs are short sayings that suggest good principles. You should learn to recognize and appreciate each of these Bible literary forms.

Short story. A literary form found in the Bible is the short story. The stories in the Bible are all true stories. An exact example of the short-story form is the book of Esther. The book of Ruth might be called a long short story. It fits the form of a novelette, but, of course, it is a true story.

To fit the short-story form, a story must have only a few main characters. Any other characters must be necessary to the action and not interesting in themselves. The time covered by the story must be brief—a few hours, a few days, or possibly two or three separated periods of time, all closely related in some way. Not much description is given, either of the looks of the characters, the look of the scenery, or the thoughts of the characters. A short story covers too brief a time to allow for describing character development. The action of the short story centers around one happening or possibly two or three closely related incidents.

Most of the short stories of the Bible have been included in the Pentateuch, the historical books of the Old Testament, and the Acts of the Apostles. Stories about the heroes of certain periods of history make history real. Especially in Bible history, stories about individuals who obeyed God or individuals who went against God's will are found. These stories make us understand that people make history.

Look for the "short stories" that are woven into the history of Israel. The one you are going to read is in Judges, Chapter 6. To follow is the story of the call of Gideon, retold in today's language.

The Call of Gideon

Gideon drew himself up to the edge of the wine press pit and looked cautiously around. Not seeing any of the **raiding** Midianites, he climbed out of the pit and stretched. Gideon was a strong young man, but threshing the wheat was back-breaking work, and hot. Gideon threshed the wheat down in the wine-press pit so that the Midianites would not see it.

As Gideon wiped the sweat and threshing dust from his face and neck, he wondered how much longer his father would stay in Ophrah in the land of Manasseh. Many of their neighbors had gone to live in dens and caves in the mountains. Some had found places in the mountains that were naturally walled-in by rocks and were easy to guard.

"Seven years!" Gideon thought, sighing. For seven years the Midianites had swarmed over the land, crossing from the east side of the Jordan River. They arrived suddenly, every harvest, thundering in on hundreds of camels. Those huge, ill-tempered beasts alone were enough to scare the Israelite farmers into helplessness. Each harvest time the Midianites pitched their tents on the farms. Each time they rounded up all of the sheep, oxen, and asses. Each time they packed up all the grain and fruit, and off they went. Neither the prayers to Jehovah nor the sacrifices to Baal, which some of the Israelites were making along with their Baal-worshiping neighbors, seemed to make any difference.

Suddenly Gideon was aware of someone sitting beneath the big oak tree near the wine press.

"The Lord is with you, you mighty man of **valour**," said the stranger.

Gideon's heart began to pound. Something was different about the man and about the greeting. Could the stranger be a prophet? No prophet had been preaching in Israel that Gideon had heard of. Nevertheless, Gideon decided, the stranger must be a prophet, so he said, "Excuse me, but if the Lord is with us, why has all this happened to us? Why do we not see miracles like the wonderful deeds the Lord did for our fathers when He brought them from Egypt? Now the Lord has thrown us aside and let the Midianites ruin us."

The stranger looked straight at Gideon and said, "Go in the strength I give you! Go and save Israel from the Midianites! Go, for I am sending you!"

Gideon was astonished at the face of the stranger—a face of holiness and power and love. Gideon was astonished at what the stranger said. Could it mean what it seemed to mean?

Scarcely able to reply, Gideon stammered, "Oh sir, how can I save Israel? My family is the poorest in the whole tribe of Manasseh, and no one thinks much of me."

"But I will be with you! And you shall destroy the Midianites as quickly as if they were one man!" was the man's reply. Now Gideon was really stunned.

Too humble to believe at once that he would really be called to save Israel, too shy to ask more questions but needing to be sure, Gideon asked the stranger to show him a sign.

Gideon also remembered his manners. No stranger should ever be allowed to leave without first being offered hospitality, and Gideon knew he should offer him food.

"Please stay here until I can go home and return with a present for you."

"I promise to stay," replied the stranger.

Hurrying home, Gideon quickly prepared the roasted young goat and the bread (there was only time for **unleavened** flat cakes). He put the meat and bread in the same basket and carried the broth in a pot. He did not want to take a servant with him. Suppose the stranger were gone? Suppose he had imagined the whole scene? How foolish he would look in front of a servant.

With relief Gideon saw that the stranger was still under the oak tree. Gideon approached and presented the food.

"Place the meat and the bread on this rock," said the stranger, pointing to a rock close at hand. "Pour the broth over the bread and meat."

Gideon obeyed, his excitement increasing all the while. His feeling that this was no ordinary stranger was growing stronger.

The man reached out with his walking staff and touched the meat and bread. Instantly fire came out of the rock and burned up the bread and the meat, wet as they were from the broth! And just as instantly the stranger disappeared!

"Oh, help me, my Lord God!," cried Gideon. "I am afraid because I have seen an angel of the Lord face to face."

Though the pounding of his heart sounded like thunder to him, Gideon could still hear the voice that said, "It is all right. Do not be afraid. You will not die."

Gideon sat down to think about the meaning of all that had happened that day. It gradually became clear to him that the Lord God had really called him to the task of saving the

Israelites from the Midianites. But he was not sure what he should do next.

After a while Gideon thought, "I will at least build an altar here where the angel of the Lord appeared to me and where God talked to me. The altar will show my Baal-worshiping neighbors that Gideon worships Jehovah, the Lord God." He set to work gathering the stones and piling them up to form an altar. "The Lord God promised me that He would use me to bring peace to my people. I will name this altar 'Jehovah's Peace,' and it will stand here as a witness."

The day was gone when Gideon had finished. Gideon was worn out with the hard work of the day and the excitement of the special thing that had happened. He ate his supper and went to bed expecting to sleep soundly.

Sometime after everyone was asleep, Gideon was suddenly wakened. The voice of the Lord God again!

"Gideon, take your father's best ox and hitch it to the altar of Baal that belongs to your father. Pull the altar of Baal down! Then cut down the heathen sacred grove next to it. Build an altar for the Lord God on the rock. Use the wood from the grove for firewood. Sacrifice the ox on the altar."

Gideon was wide awake and ready to go by the time the orders were given. "I won't wait until daylight," he thought. "The men of the city will be furious. If I wait until daylight, I might not even be able to do it."

As quietly as he could, Gideon awakened ten of his men servants and told them the plan. Silently they harnessed the ox and placed the ropes around the altar. Praying that the people of the city would be kept soundly asleep, Gideon urged the ox forward. Down tumbled the altar.

Setting some of his men to cutting down the grove, Gideon with the others quickly built a new altar to the Lord God. Then, with his men gathered around, Gideon witnessed to his trust in the Lord God by sacrificing the ox on the altar.

Daylight was greeted by shouts of, "Who did it? Who pulled down the altar of Baal?"

That kind of secret does not stay secret long, and soon a **delegation** of men from the city were at the door of Gideon's father, Joash.

"Bring him out, Joash. Bring Gideon out. We are going to kill him for tearing down Baal's altar and cutting down our sacred grove."

Joash stood in the door and **mocked** them, "Do you have to take care of Baal? If Baal is a god, let him take care of himself. Let Baal handle it if someone pulls down his altar."

And that was the end of that matter—but just the beginning of the wonderful things God had planned for Gideon. Gideon did indeed rid the land of the Midianites. The stories of his **exploits** are written in Bible history and his faith has been mentioned many times over the centuries.

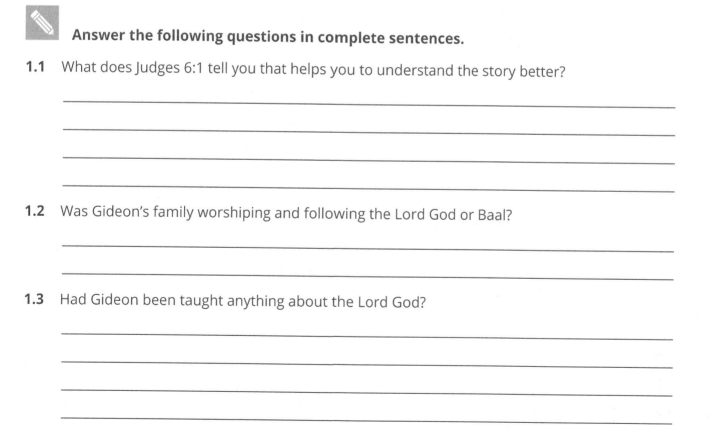

Answer the following questions in complete sentences.

1.1   What does Judges 6:1 tell you that helps you to understand the story better?

_____

_____

_____

_____

1.2   Was Gideon's family worshiping and following the Lord God or Baal?

_____

_____

1.3   Had Gideon been taught anything about the Lord God?

_____

_____

_____

_____

Fill in the guide to the story about Gideon.

1.4   I. Setting:

_____

_____

_____

II. Characters:

A. Main characters: _____

B. Other characters: _____

III. Action: _____

_____

_____

_____

_____

_____

_____

_____

_____

_____

_____

_____

_____

_____

_____

_____

Review what you read about what makes a short story and answer *yes* if the story about Gideon followed the measures of a short story.

1.5   _____   Few main characters

1.6   _____   Short time covered

1.7   _____   Not much description

1.8   _____   Action centers around one happening or two or three closely related happenings

Parable. A parable is a short teaching story. The story compares something to something else in order to help people see relationships or consequences. Some form of parable has been known among almost all peoples of the world. The Israelites knew parables that were something like the Greek fables. Jotham, the youngest son of Gideon, told one such parable to warn the men who had killed his brothers. Jotham's parable is recorded in Judges 9:8–15.

In the parable Jotham told, he compared the men of Shechem and Millo to trees and the man they had chosen as king to a rough, thorny shrub. He compared the better men they might have chosen to be king to the olive tree, to the fig three, and to the grape vine. All of these are useful plants, but the thorny shrub is useful only to start a fire.

Sometimes parables are explained, sometimes they are not. Jotham explained his parable to mean that trouble would come from Abimelech, who had been chosen king. He said fire would come from Abimelech and devour the people of Shechem and Millo. The rest of Judges chapter 9 tells what kind of trouble actually happened.

The parables of the New Testament are better known. Jesus used parables frequently throughout his teaching ministry. Jesus' parables were somewhat different from Old Testament parables. Jesus' parables always had special meaning that could only be known to those who had spiritual understanding. Often Jesus explained the spiritual meaning to His disciples when they were away from the crowd.

 Read the following Bible passages and write the parable that each passage records.

1.9 2 Samuel 12:1–4 _____

1.10 2 Kings 14:9 _____

1.11 Isaiah 5:1–7 _____

1.12 Matthew 13:3–9 _____

1.13 Mark 2:21 _____

1.14 Luke 20:9–16 _____

Proverb. Proverbs are a form of Hebrew verse. Proverbs are not poetry in the same way psalms are. Proverbs have the characteristic of Hebrew verse that is called **parallelism**.
Read this proverb (Proverbs 15:1).

"A soft answer turneth away wrath:
but grievous words stir up anger."

Notice these things: (1) the proverb is in two parallel parts; (2) two contrasting things are the subjects of the two parts (soft answer and grievous words); and (3) different words are used for the same thing in the predicates (wrath and anger). Sometimes the second part of the proverb explains or **intensifies** the first part.

Open your Bible to any chapter of Proverbs and notice how frequently this pattern is followed. Parallelism is a literary device used by the Hebrew writers to help people remember. Every people has its own proverbs. The Hebrew proverbs belong to Christians as well as to the Hebrews because God caused them to be written down for our benefit, too.

Match the parallel parts of the proverbs.

1.15 _____ A faithful witness will not lie:

1.16 _____ A wise son heareth his father's instruction:

1.17 _____ Better is a dry morsel and quietness therewith,

1.18 _____ A friend loveth at all times,

1.19 _____ There is a way that seemeth right to a man,

1.20 _____ Favour is deceitful, and beauty is vain:

1.21 _____ The wise shall inherit glory: of fools.

a. than a house full of sacrifices with strife.

b. but the end thereof are the ways of death.

c. for out of it are the issues of life.

d. but a false witness will utter lies.

e. but a woman that feareth the Lord, she shall be praised.

f. but a scorner heareth not rebuke.

g. and a brother is born for adversity.

h. but shame shall be the promotion of fools.

Complete the following statements.

1.22 A short story that teaches by comparing something to something else is a _____ .

1.23 A short, wise saying is a _____ .

1.24 In the Bible parables may be found in both the a. _____ and the b. _____ .

1.25 The time covered in a short story is _____ .

1.26 Short stories have _____ main characters.

1.27 The short-story form may be found in the Pentateuch, the

a. _____ and the

b. _____ .

REPORT WRITING

In this section you will learn the beginning steps of writing a report, and make preparations for a report that you will write on a Bible topic. You will learn how to choose a topic and where to find information.

Study each section carefully. If you can learn to follow these beginning steps, it will help you write a good report. Though it may not seem like it, these steps will actually save you time!

Choosing a topic. Sometimes a topic is given to you so you do not have a choice. Other times you must choose the topic yourself. Here are some guidelines for you to follow.

1. Make a list of topics. Sometimes you may sit and think and think and think. You cannot think of a topic. Try looking through some encyclopedias or reference books. Something may catch your eye and give you an idea for a general topic.

Be sure to choose a topic that most interests you from your list. Then the report will be more enjoyable to you and also to your readers or listeners.

2. Do not make your topic too broad. Maybe you have looked through some books and have decided you would like to report on mammals. However, a topic like mammals would be too broad or too general. You could write a book on mammals, but all you want to write is a report! Make your topic more **specific**. Choose a topic about some feature of mammals or choose a specific mammal.

Read this list of specific topics about mammals.

- Characteristics of Mammals
- Animals of Speed
- Animals with Pouches
- Whales-Are They Becoming Extinct?
- Australia's Wild Dogs
- Facts and Legends about Hyenas

Complete this activity.

1.28 Read this list of topics. Underline the three topics that are too broad or general. Circle two or three topics that interest you.

REPORT TOPICS	
Rocky Mountain Goats	Solomon's Temple
How Steel is Made	Kangaroos
Legends about Robin Hood	Astronomy
The Bible	Animals in the Bible
How Igneous Rocks are Formed	Weather Forecasting
Hunting the Whale	Effects of Pollution on Fish
Hurricanes	Birds
Egyptian Pyramids	

In Section 3 of this LIFEPAC, you will actually write a report on a Bible topic. It will be important for you to follow carefully the steps that are presented in each section. The first step for you to take in Section 1 is to choose a topic.

You have already read the steps in choosing a topic: (1) Make a list of topics, and (2) Do not make your topics too broad. Remember to use the Bible or Bible-related books and magazines to **stimulate** your thinking. A topical Bible or concordance may also be helpful in selecting a topic.

Complete this activity.

1.29 Read the following Bible topics. Write some of your own ideas for topics on the blanks. Talk with your parents, teacher, and/or pastor about possible topics.

BIBLE TOPICS		
salvation	Pauls first missionary journey	Esther
sin	Jericho	early church
heaven	idolatry	Job
prayer		love
_____	_____	_____

Choose a Bible topic for your report. Write it on the blank.

1.30 My topic is _____ .

TEACHER CHECK _____ _____

initials   date

Gathering information. After you decide on a topic, the next step is to find information. Your topic choice will determine where you go for information.

For instance, if you choose a topic such as "Training to Be a Missionary," you may get information from a book on missionaries, the Bible, or you may interview a missionary or talk to your pastor.

Sometimes you may get all the information you need from one source, and at other times you may have to consult several sources. Read this list of some of the sources of information.

SOURCES OF INFORMATION	
encyclopedias	books on the topic
magazines	Bible
yourself	interviews
Internet resources	

Complete this activity.

1.31 Read each topic. Decide where you would look for information. Write one or two sources of information below each topic. Use of the list of sources of information.

a. Solomon's Temple

_____

b. Your home town

_____

c. Kangaroos

_____

Complete this activity.

1.32 Find a source or sources of information about your choice of a Bible topic. Write the source or sources of information you will use on the blanks.

_____

_____

TEACHER CHECK _____ _____
initials   date

SPELLING AND HANDWRITING

In this section you will learn to spell two-, three-, and four-syllable words. You will improve your skill in writing difficult letters.

Spelling. Dividing words into syllables is a valuable skill for better spelling. Syllables are like small words or sound groups within the word. Learn to spell each group correctly, put them together, and you have learned to spell the word.

Your spelling list consists of two-, three-, and four-syllable words. Listen for each syllable in every word as you study and write it.

Learn to spell the words from Spelling Words-1.

SPELLING WORDS-1

automatic	hero	participate
cereal	inheritance	poem
chariot	manufacture	relationship
composition	mechanical	sofa
congratulate	memorial	stanza
continual	menu	zero
creation	museum	

Copy the spelling words in your best handwriting.

1.33 Spelling Words-1

a. _____   b. _____

c. _____   d. _____

e. _____   f. _____

g. _____   h. _____

i. _____   j. _____

k. _____   l. _____

m. _____   n. _____

o. _____   p. _____

q. _____   r. _____

s. _____   t. _____

Complete the following activities. You may use your dictionary.

1.34 Write the three words which end in a vowel and have the syllable division after a long vowel. Divide each word into syllables.

Example: mo / tel

a. _____   b. _____   c. _____

1.35 Write the one word which ends in a vowel with the syllable division between two consonants. Divide the word into syllables.

_____

1.36 Write the one word which ends in a vowel and the first syllable is "men." Divide the word into syllables.

_____

1.37 Write the one two-syllable word and four three-syllable words where there is one syllable division between two vowels.

Divide the words into syllables.

Example: flu / id

a. _____   b. _____   c. _____

d. _____   e. _____

1.38 Complete the following four-syllable words to match the correct definition. Divide each word into syllables.

a. _____ -ance   a. Received as an heir.

b. _____ -late   b. Express one's pleasure at the happiness of someone.

c. _____ -al

d. _____ -ture   c. Never stopping; repeated many times.

e. _____ -pate   d. Making articles by hand or machine.

f. _____ -ic   e. Take part.

g. _____ -tion   f. Moving or acting by itself.

h. _____ -al   g. The making up of anything; the putting together of a whole.

i. _____ -ship   h Something that is a reminder.

j. _____ -cal   i. Connection.

                                          j. Having to do with machinery.

1.39 Read the following verses in your Bible. Write one word from each verse that is a spelling word.

a. Mark 13:19   _____

b. Colossians 1:12   _____

c. 2 Kings 2:11   _____

1.40 Solve the minipuzzle.

Down
1. brave person
3. verse of a poem

Across
2. nothing
3. couch
4. list of food

1.41 Write a sentence for each of the following words.

a. poem _____

b. cereal _____

c. museum _____

TEACHER CHECK _____ _____
initials   date

ABC **Ask your teacher to give you a practice spelling test of Spelling Words-1.** Restudy the words you missed.

Handwriting. Review the shapes of the letters *s* and *r*.

This _____   Not this _____

✎ **Complete the following handwriting activities.**

1.42 Practice writing the letters *s* and *r*.

_s_   _r_

1.43 Copy the following words. Be sure to form each *s* and *r* correctly.

sister   *rich*   *sat*

Mississippi   *rushing*

messy   *sassy*

rainy   *river*   *Mary*

1.44 Write a few silly sentences in your best handwriting. Use the practice words and add a few of your own.

↺ **Review the material in this section in preparation for the Self Test.** This Self Test will check your mastery of this particular section. The items missed on this Self Test will indicate specific areas where restudy is needed for mastery.

SELF TEST 1

Write true or false (each answer, 2 points).

1.01 _____ Short stories are found in the Bible.

1.02 _____ Proverbs are long poems.

1.03 _____ Parables are very similar to proverbs.

1.04 _____ Parables are found in the New Testament and the Old Testament.

1.05 _____ Short stories have long, involved descriptions.

1.06 _____ Short stories in the Bible are true.

1.07 _____ Parables are always explained.

1.08 _____ A topic for a written report should be specific.

1.09 _____ You should always use just one source for a report.

1.010 _____ Your topic choices will decide where you will go for information.

Write the letter of the correct match (each answer, 2 points).

1.011 _____ is a short teaching story.

1.012 _____ is characteristic of Hebrew verse used in Proverbs.

1.013 _____ was an idol.

1.014 _____ should interest you.

1.015 _____ are short sayings that suggest good principles.

1.016 _____ are brief in time.

1.017 _____ rid the land of Midianites.

1.018 _____ often used parables.

1.019 _____ is an example of a short story.

1.020 _____ consists of the first five books of the Old Testament.

a. The book of Esther

b. Proverbs

c. Parable

d. Gideon

e. Parallelism

f. Pentateuch

g. The angel of the Lord

h. Jesus

i. Short stories

j. A topic choice

k. Baal

Complete the following statements (each answer, 3 points).

1.021 An example of a literary form included in the Pentateuch and in the Acts of the Apostles is the _____ .

1.022 Jotham's comparison of the men of Shechem and Millo to trees and the man they had chosen as king to a rough, thorny bush is an example of a _____ .

1.023 Parallelism is a literary device found in _____ .

1.024 The topic, *Animals of the World*, would be too _____ .

1.025 Short stories have _____ main characters.

1.026 A good source of information for a Bible topic would be the _____ .

1.027 A _____ compares something to something else in order to help people see relationships or consequences.

1.028 _____ are not poetry in the same way the psalms are.

1.029 The Hebrew proverbs belong to _____ as well as to the Hebrews.

1.030 "...Holy men of _____ spake as they were moved by the Holy Ghost."

Write the letter of the correct answer on the blank (each answer, 2 points).

1.031 The story of Gideon is an example of a _____ .
a. short story   b. parable   c. proverb

1.032 A short story has a setting, characters, and _____ .
a. a moral   b. parallelism   c. action

1.033 Gideon must have been taught something about the Lord God because _____ .
a. he was Jewish
b. he saw the angel of the Lord and cried to the Lord God for help
c. he was hiding from the raiding Midianites

1.034 The passage in the New Testament telling of new cloth sewn onto old cloth is an example of a _____ .
a. proverb   b. short story   c. parable

1.035 "A soft answer turneth away wrath: but grievous words stir up anger" is an example of a _____ .
a. proverb   b. psalm   c. parable

1.036 "The wise shall inherit glory:" is parallel to _____ .
a. "for out of it are the issues of life."
b. "but shame shall be the promotion of fools."
c. "but a false witness will utter lies."

1.037 "The wicked flee when no man pursueth:" is parallel to _____ .
   a. "but the righteous are bold as a lion."
   b. "but a child left to himself bringeth his mother to shame."
   c. "but a woman that feareth the Lord, she shall be praised."

1.038 An example of a topic that is too broad is _____ .
   a. Hurricanes   b. Animals of Speed   c. The Bible

1.039 An example of a specific topic is _____ .
   a. Birds of the World   b. Mars   c. Astronomy

1.040 A good source of information for a report on *Hunting Whales* is _____ .
   a. an encyclopedia   b. A Christian magazine   c. a craft book

Answer the following questions (each answer, 5 points).

1.041 What are two characteristics of a short story?

_____

_____

_____

_____

1.042 What is the first step in writing a report and how would you go about it?

_____

_____

_____

_____

_____

_____

_____

_____

80/100   **SCORE** _____   **TEACHER** _____ _____
                                        initials   date

ABC **Take your spelling test of Spelling Words-1.**

2. SECTION TWO

"The heavens declare the glory of God; and the firmament sheweth his handiwork."

This verse does not rhyme but it will match any poetry in the world for beauty of expression and majesty of thought. In this section you will learn about the Hebrew poetic form and the forms in which prophecy was given. You will learn how to take notes and organize your material into an outline for a written report. You will learn how to spell more multisyllable words and practice writing certain difficult letters correctly.

Section Objectives

Review these objectives. When you have completed this section, you should be able to:

1. Identify seven Bible literary forms.
5. Describe the main characteristics of Hebrew poetry.
6. Describe the main characteristics of Hebrew prophecy.
7. Take notes for a written report.
8. Identify the purpose of writing a report.
9. Outline notes for a written report.
13. Spell new words correctly.
14. Correctly form letters.

Vocabulary

Study these words to enhance your learning success in this section.

convince (kun vins'). Persuade firmly.

exalted (eg zôl' tud). Filled with joy or a noble feeling.

intense (in tens'). Very great or strong.

lament (lu ment'). Weep; sorrow.

projection (pru jek' shun). Part that sticks out.

species (spē shēz). Group of animals that have certain permanent characteristics in common.

utterances (ut' ur uns es). Expressing in words or sounds.

Pronunciation Key: hat, āge, cãre, fär; let, ēqual, tėrm; it, īce; hot, ōpen, ôrder; oil; out; cup, pu̇t, rüle; child; long; thin; /ŦH/ for then; /zh/ for measure; /u/ or /ə/ represents /a/ in about, /e/ in taken, /i/ in pencil, /o/ in lemon, and /u/ in circus.

BIBLE POETRY AND PROPHECY

The psalms come to mind first when Bible poetry is mentioned. The book called *The Psalms* is a collection of poetry of the Israelites. One-third of the Bible, however, was actually composed in poetic form. Bible prophecy also is not limited to the books that are labeled *Prophetic Books*, but most prophecy is found in these books. In this section you will study the elements of Hebrew poetry and gain some appreciation of it. You will also learn the meaning of the term *prophecy* as used in the Bible and the characteristics of the prophecy in the Bible.

Poetry. Most translations of the Bible do not print the poetry passages of the Bible as poetry, not even the Psalms. Scholars have learned, however, that the following books of the Bible were written entirely in poetic form. Learn the names of these books.

The Psalms	Lamentations	Nahum
Proverbs	Obadiah	Habakkuk
Song of Solomon	Micah	Zephaniah

In addition, large parts of Job, Isaiah, Hosea, Joel, and Amos were written in the poetic form. About one-half of Jeremiah is poetic in form. Only Leviticus, Ruth, Ezra, Nehemiah, Esther, Haggai, and Malachi of the Old Testament books do not contain some poetic lines.

Although the New Testament does not have any single book that may be classified as poetry, poetry does have a place in the New Testament. Some portions of the New Testament writings are poetical because the language is **exalted**, and the reader feels lifted up toward God. Some bits of Old Testament poetry are quoted, as well as parts of ancient hymns.

The Hebrew poetry of the Bible shares some characteristics with other kinds of poetry, yet is distinctly different. Hebrew poetry has cadence—the musical quality that belongs to all poetry. Hebrew poetry expresses thoughts and feelings that are common to everyone in a way that most people cannot express them. That, too, is a characteristic common to all poetry. Hebrew poetry, like other poetry, uses simile and metaphor, but unlike English poetry, few adjectives. Some poetry has *meter*, which is a certain number of unstressed syllables for every stressed syllable; Hebrew poetry does not have meter. Some poetry rhymes; Hebrew poetry never rhymes.

An interesting feature of some of the psalms and some of the proverbs is that they are written in acrostic form. Acrostics are made when the first letter of each line or verse is a letter of the alphabet or when the first letters spell the word that is the subject of the verses. The Hebrew acrostic cannot be seen in the English translation, but Psalm 119 is an example of the acrostic form.

The most important element of Hebrew poetry is the poetic device of parallelism. Parallelism in poetry means that two closely related thoughts are set opposite each other in such a way that they balance. The best way to understand this idea is to study some examples of different kinds of balance in Hebrew poetry taken from Psalm 19.

> *"The heavens declare the glory of God;*
> *and the firmament sheweth his handiwork."*

"Heavens" and "firmament" mean the same thing. The second part repeats the idea of the first part but develops it a little differently. "God's glory" is shown in "His handiwork."

> *"Day unto day uttereth speech,*
> *and night unto night sheweth knowledge."*

In this verse each part of the compound sentence follows the same sentence pattern, that is, they are parallel. A partial contrast in idea is brought in—"day" and "night" are contrasted. Both day and night do the same thing that the heavens do—tell of an element of God's glory.

"The law of the Lord is perfect, converting the soul: the testimony of the Lord is sure, making wise the simple. The statutes of the Lord are right, rejoicing the heart: the commandment of the Lord is pure, enlightening the eyes. The fear of the Lord is clean, enduring for ever: the judgments of the Lord are true and righteous all together."

In these verses something is added with each new part, building the idea of the perfection of God's law higher and higher.

Much of the poetry of the Old Testament was meant to be sung. King David composed many of the psalms for singing in worship services. First Chronicles chapters 15 and 16 has an account of the day when King David brought the Ark of the Covenant to the tent he had prepared for it in the city of David. At that time, the account says (1 Chronicles 15:16), David asked the chief of the Levites to appoint certain Levites (Asaph and others) to be "...the singers with instruments of musick, psalteries and harps and cymbals, sounding, by lifting up the voice with joy." On that same day David delivered to Asaph a psalm of thanksgiving (16:7). The psalm is recorded in verses 8–36. It is recorded, with some changes, in the book of the Psalms as Psalm 105.

| Statue of King David

Complete the following activities.

2.1 List the nine books of the Old Testament that were written entirely in the poetic form.

a. _____ b. _____ c. _____

d. _____ e. _____ f. _____

g. _____ h. _____ i. _____

2.2 Name the Old Testament book that has half of its verses in poetry. _____

2.3   List the seven books of the Old Testament that have no lines of poetry in them.

a. _____   b. _____   c. _____

d. _____   e. _____   f. _____

g. _____

Memorize the following verses.

2.4   Memorize Psalm 19:1–6. When you have memorized them, say them with meaningful expression to a friend.

FRIEND CHECK _____ _____

initials   date

The New Testament does not have as much poetry as the Old Testament, but it has some very beautiful passages. Eight of them are found in Luke chapters 1 and 2.

Read the following verses from Luke: 1:14–17, 32, 33, 35, 46–55, 68–79; 2:14, 29–32, 34, and 35.

Complete the following activity. Read the Bible passages. Write on the blank whether the passage is *poetry* or *not poetry*.

2.5   _____   Genesis 49:23–26

2.6   _____   Exodus 15:1–3

2.7   _____   Exodus 26:1

2.8   _____   Numbers 6:24–26

2.9   _____   Judges 5:2 and 3

2.10   _____   Jonah 2:2–9

2.11   _____   Haggai 1:7–9

2.12   _____   Matthew 4:15–17

2.13   _____   Matthew 21:5

2.14   _____   Acts 2:17–21

2.15   _____   Romans 9:25 and 26

2.16   _____   Hebrews 12:5 and 6

You have learned that poetry may be found in most of the books of the Bible. In addition to the passages that are identified as actual poetry, many passages of poetic prose are in the Bible. Learn to look for and enjoy the poetic prose of the Bible. You will recognize poetic passages because of their **intense** or exalted expression. In the New Testament read these passages that are examples of beautiful poetic prose.

1. the Beatitudes (Matthew 5:3–12)

2. Jesus' **lament** over Jerusalem (Matthew 23:37–39)

3. the exalted promise of victory (Romans 8:31–39)

4. the wonderful love chapter (1 Corinthians chapter 13)

5. the Benediction (Jude verses 24 and 25)

 Answer these questions.

2.17 What is the poetic device in the Beatitudes? _____

2.18 What simile is used in Jesus' lament over Jerusalem? _____

_____

2.19 In the exalted promise of victory in Romans 8:31–39, what causes the intensity of feeling to

build up? _____

_____

_____

2.20 In the love chapter of 1 Corinthians 13, what poetic devices can you find?

_____

2.21 In the Benediction (the last two verses of Jude), what makes the passage poetic?

_____

_____

Prophetic writing. Prophetic writing is mainly the record of **utterances** by prophets. These were written down afterwards, either by the prophet or by a scribe. Six of the nine books written entirely in poetry are prophetic books. Most of the prophetic writing that is not poetry is poetic prose. The reason is not hard to find. Prophecy always involves an intensity of emotion. Poetry and poetic prose are the natural way to express emotion.

As a literary form prophetic writing is unique to the Bible. Within the prophetic writings are to be found stories, parables, history, and biography as well as poetry. You will remember from Bible studies that the prophet was not only one who *foretold*, although he often foretold what was to happen. The Hebrew prophet was also one who *told forth* the message of God. The prophet was God's "mouth" to Israel. Elisha was called "the man of God." This title is used for him thirty-six times.

What God said to Israel he said to their hearts as well as to their heads. Prophetic writing and the recording of prophetic utterances, therefore, have in them all of the kinds of writing that will move people to do the right things and to have greater faith and love toward God.

Not all prophetic writing is found in the books of the Bible known as *The Prophets* or *prophetic writings*. Many people, better known in other ways, also made prophetic utterances from time to time.

David wrote prophetic psalms as well as worship psalms.

Moses, the great leader of the Israelites, was also a prophet.

Isaac, when he gave his death-bed blessing to his sons, made prophetic utterances about the future of Israel.

Often the prophetic writings contained hidden meanings. Figurative language was used in prophetic writing. This does not mean that all prophetic writing is figurative and never has a literal meaning. All prophecy must be studied under the direction of the Holy Spirit. The study of prophecy itself belongs to Bible study. This LIFEPAC is only concerned with the literary form of prophecy.

 Read Zechariah 9:9–17 and do the following activities.

2.22 Find at least five of the eight similes.

a. _____

b. _____

c. _____

d. _____

e. _____

2.23 Find four of the six parallel phrases or sentences.

a. _____
_____

b. _____
_____

c. _____
_____

d. _____
_____

2.24 What is the prophetic message of this passage?

_____

_____

2.25 What is the New Testament fulfillment of verse 9?

_____

_____

REPORT WRITING

You have learned how to begin a report by choosing a topic and finding sources of information. Now you will learn how to take notes from the information and how to write an outline from the notes.

Taking notes. The first step in taking notes is to decide what you want to know about your topic. It is a good idea to write down some questions you would like answered in your report.

Read the following questions for a report on kangaroos.

Questions

Where do kangaroos live?

How big are they?

Are there different kinds of kangaroos?

_____

_____

_____

_____

_____

 Complete this activity.

2.26 Think of at least two more questions about kangaroos that you would like answered. Write them in the question box.

LANGUAGE ARTS 609

LIFEPAC TEST

NAME _____

DATE _____

SCORE _____

LANGUAGE ARTS 609: LIFEPAC TEST

Write true or false (each answer, 2 points).

1. _____ Since penalties are imposed for breaking the law, the law must be easily understood.

2. _____ No historical writings occur in the New Testament books.

3. _____ Ceremonial law governed all parts of Hebrew life.

4. _____ The four Gospels are largely biographical.

5. _____ Parables only occur in the Old Testament.

6. _____ Short stories in the Bible are fiction just like all short stories.

7. _____ Hebrew poetry never rhymes.

8. _____ You do not need any special direction to study prophecy.

9. _____ Hebrew poetry has parallelism.

10. _____ Hebrew prophecy is unique to the Bible.

Write the letter of the correct match (each answer, 2 points).

11. _____ is a systematic collection of laws.

12. _____ is an example of a short story in the Bible.

13. _____ in an outline should be related to the main topics.

14. _____ are found more frequently in the New Testament than the Old Testament.

15. _____ belong to Christians as well as the Hebrew people.

16. _____ have short descriptions.

17. _____ are also called the Decalogue.

18. _____ spoke as they were moved by the Holy Spirit.

19. _____ is a good source for report material on some subjects.

20. _____ is the first step in report writing.

a. Hebrew proverbs

b. Short stories

c. Holy men of God

d. The story of Gideon

e. Draft

f. Parables

g. The Ten Commandments

h. An encyclopedia

i. A code

j. Choosing a topic

k. Subtopics

Complete the following statements (each answer, 3 points).

21. The basic commandments are the Decalogue or the _____ .

22. Many of the nonhistorical books contain incidental pieces of _____ .

23. "Thou shalt have no other gods before me," is an example of a _____ .

24. The three main parts of an outline are main topics, _____ , and details.

25. Outlining helps you _____ information for a report.

26. Three main purposes for writing a report are to entertain, _____ , and convince.

27. A short story has _____ , setting, and characters.

28. _____ should be written only as main ideas in your own words.

29. Prophecy often contains _____ meanings.

30. The Hebrew proverbs belong to _____ as well as to the Hebrews.

31. The last three steps in writing a report are drafting, _____ , and finalizing.

Write the letter of the correct answer on the blank (each answer, 2 points).

32. The laws given to Moses by God are called the _____ .
    a. covenant   b. Mosaic Law   c. Promise

33. "Thou shalt not take the name of the Lord thy God in vain" is an example of a _____ .
    a. commandment   b. proverb   c. psalm

34. "A man's pride shall bring him low: but honour shall uphold the humble in spirit," is an example of a _____ .
    a. psalm   b. prophecy   c. proverb

35. The Beatitudes are an example of _____ .
    a. a parable   b. poetic prose   c. proverbs

36. The psalms are an example of _____ .
    a. Hebrew poetry   b. poetic prose   c. prophecy

37. First Chronicles is one of the historical books of the _____ .
    a. Acts of the Apostles   b. New Testament   c. Old Testament

38. "He that gathereth in summer is a wise son" is parallel to _____ .
    a. "the Lord is the maker of them all."
    b. "but the hand of the diligent maketh rich."
    c. "but he that sleepeth in harvest is a son that causeth shame."

39. An example of a specific topic is _____ .
    a. Solomon's Temple   b. Mammals   c. the Universe

40. "...As a hen gathereth her chickens under her wings" is an example of a _____ .
a. metaphor   b. simile   c. parallelism

Define the following words (each definition, 2 points).

41. parallelism _____

_____

42. parable _____

_____

43. proverb _____

_____

44. history _____

_____

45. poetic prose _____

_____

ABC **Take your LIFEPAC Spelling Test.**

As you begin to take notes, keep in mind the purpose of your report. Will you be writing your report to entertain, inform, or **convince**? You may have just one purpose or several.

A report on the "Legends of Robin Hood" may entertain and inform.

A report on the "effects of pollution on fish" may inform and convince.

The report may convince others of the harmful effects of pollution.

A report on "kangaroos" may just inform.

With questions and your purpose in mind, your are ready to begin reading your information and to take notes. You take notes to help you remember. Write only the main ideas that answer your questions and fulfill your purpose. In other words, do not write everything.

Read this list of helpful hints for note-taking.

- Put your notes on cards.
- Write only the main ideas.
- Write the main ideas in your own words.
- Don't write in complete sentences.
- Write where you got the information on the card so you can check back if you need to do so (title, author, and page number).

On the next page you will learn more about the kangaroo family. Look for information that could go on a note card.

| A grey kangaroo

Wallabies are small kangaroos about the size of a rabbit. The size determines what they are called. If they are larger, they are called kangaroos.

The family name of kangaroos is *macropodidae* which means "great feet." Wallabies and kangaroos have large, long hind feet. This gives them the ability to hop and to leap great distances. Their large, long tails are powerful. The kangaroo tail is used to balance and prop the animal.

Large numbers of wallabies live in New Guinea and Australia. Most of the wallabies live on the open plains. They do not burrow in the ground like rabbits, but they do lie in "forms" or depressions in the ground made from using it constantly and wearing the ground down. Other wallabies live in rocks and in the brush.

Wallabies are like rabbits in that they eat grass, leaves, and similar types of vegetation. They are grey or brown and can travel at great speeds.

The habits of wallabies vary. Some wallabies live in colonies and others live alone. Some come out only at night, and others are out feeding during the day.

A Banded Wallaby has eleven or twelve short stripes across his back. The Nail-tailed Wallaby has a nail-like **projection** on the tip of its tail. The Rock Wallaby has well padded feet to prevent it from slipping on the rocks.

Captain James Cook was a famous English explorer. He voyaged around the world during 1768 to 1771. He recorded many of his discoveries.

On this long voyage, he was sailing along the coast of eastern Australia. His ship sprang a leak and he had to find a harbor quickly. While repairing the ship, many of his men went ashore to explore the land. They saw an animal they described as being a mouse-color, slim, and very fast. Captain Cook asked an aborigine what the animal was called.

He answered, "kangaroo" which meant "I don't know" in his language. However, that has been the name of the animal ever since.

Another kind of kangaroo lives in the trees. Its hind limbs are not as long, but they are still built for hopping. Its foot pads are rougher to help it climb better. The tree kangaroo is about four feet long including its tail.

The Musk Kangaroo is the smallest of the **species**, only eighteen inches long including the tail. The Musk Kangaroo is shy like most kangaroos. It likes to eat insects, roots, fruits, and berries.

The Rat Kangaroo is very similar-looking to a rat, but is the size of a rabbit.

The most common kangaroo to most people is the Great Kangaroo. It is the largest of all the kangaroos. It lives in the plains. The Great Kangaroo may grow to be five or seven feet tall. It can weigh up to two hundred pounds. The female kangaroo is smaller.

These kangaroos can jump up to ten feet at a time. When traveling fast, they can clear fifteen or twenty feet at a time.

Kangaroos live about fifteen years. They move about with no permanent home. Once they were hunted for their meat, and gloves and boots were made from their hide. Kangaroos are harder to find now and they do not travel in the great herds of the pioneer days in Australia.

A baby kangaroo is raised in the mother's pouch for six months. It is called a "joey." Usually, only one baby is raised at a time. As it grows older, the baby looks out of the pouch as the mother hops along, sometimes at twenty-five miles an hour.

Kangaroos are usually gentle. They like to bathe in the river and also sunbathe.

Now read these notes taken from the selection on kangaroos.

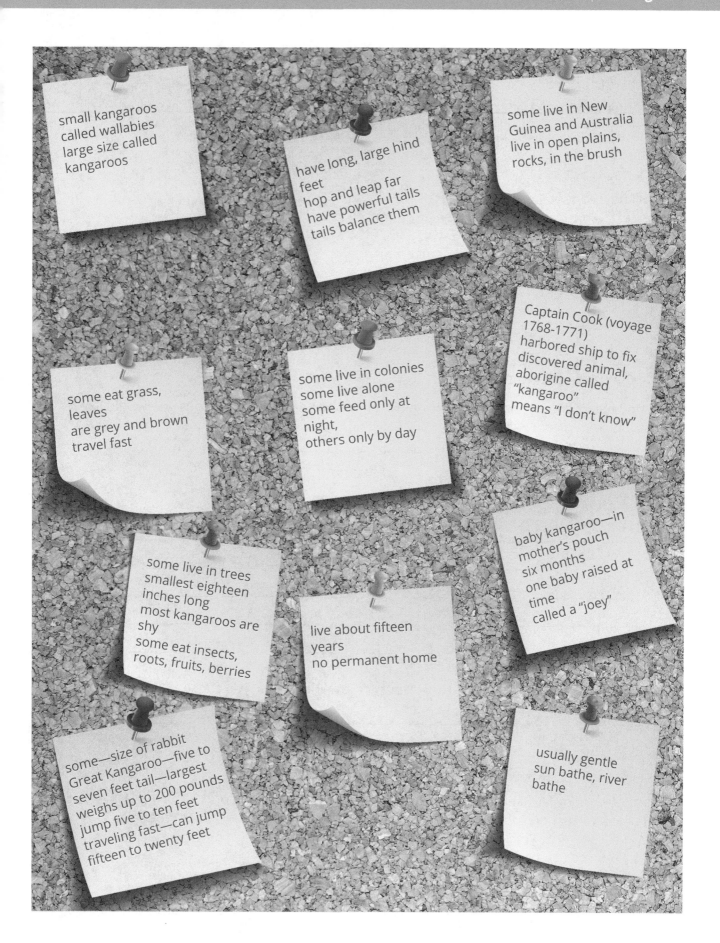

small kangaroos
called wallabies
large size called
kangaroos

have long, large hind
feet
hop and leap far
have powerful tails
tails balance them

some live in New
Guinea and Australia
live in open plains,
rocks, in the brush

some eat grass,
leaves
are grey and brown
travel fast

some live in colonies
some live alone
some feed only at
night,
others only by day

Captain Cook (voyage
1768-1771)
harbored ship to fix
discovered animal,
aborigine called
"kangaroo"
means "I don't know"

some live in trees
smallest eighteen
inches long
most kangaroos are
shy
some eat insects,
roots, fruits, berries

live about fifteen
years
no permanent home

baby kangaroo—in
mother's pouch
six months
one baby raised at
time
called a "joey"

some—size of rabbit
Great Kangaroo—five to
seven feet tail—largest
weighs up to 200 pounds
jump five to ten feet
traveling fast—can jump
fifteen to twenty feet

usually gentle
sun bathe, river
bathe

Complete this activity.

2.27 Underline the sentences or sentence parts from which each note was taken in the selection on kangaroos. Notice the information that was left out.

You will now continue preparations for your report on a Bible topic. Before you begin taking notes, think of some questions you would like answered in your report. You will also need to decide on the purpose of your report. It is to entertain, inform, or convince?

Complete these activities.

2.28 Write your choice of a Bible topic on the blank. Write several questions you would like answered in your report.

_____

My topic

Questions about my topic

_____

_____

_____

_____

_____

2.29 Write your purpose for writing the report on the Bible topic you chose.

_____

You are now ready to take notes from the sources of information you found in Section 2 of this LIFEPAC. Write your notes on a set of three-by-five-inch cards or cut enough paper that size on which to take your notes.

Review the hints for note-taking. Have your teacher check your notes when you are finished.

Check the list. Use your complete note cards.

2.30 _____ I put my notes on cards.

_____ I wrote only the main ideas on the cards.

_____ I did not write in complete sentences.

_____ I wrote the source of my information on each card.

_____ I had my teacher check my notes.

TEACHER CHECK _____ _____
initials   date

Outlining. After you have taken notes from your source or sources, study your notes and decide the best way to put them together. Outlining helps you to organize your information for a report.

If you have put your notes on cards, it will be much easier to organize the information.

Divide your report into three or four parts, called *main topics*. Three main topics on kangaroos could be *what kangaroos look like, where kangaroos live,* and *how kangaroos live.*

The main topics of the outline are divided into *subtopics*. Under the subtopics are listed more ideas called *details.*

Be sure all your information is related to the main topics.

Study the following outline. The main topics are numbered with Roman numerals (I, II, III). The subtopics are lettered with capital letters (A, B, C). The details are numbered (1, 2, 3).

Outline

Kangaroos

main topic ————→ I. What Kangaroos Look Like

    A. Size

        1. Wallabies — small

        2. Large animals called kangaroos

        3. Smallest kind, eighteen inches

        4. _____

        5. Largest — five to seven feet tall, Weighs up to two

                hundred pounds

subtopic ————→ B. Shape and color

        1. Long, large hind feet

details ————→   2. Powerful tails for balance

        3. _____

    C. Characteristics

        1. Usually shy and gentle

        2. Hop and leap far — large hop five to ten feet —

                when going fast can leap from fifteen to twenty feet

II. Where Kangaroos Live

    A. Native to New Guineas and Australia

    B. Land kangaroos

        1. In open plains

        2. _____

        3. In the brush

        4. No permanent homes

    C. Tree kangaroos

III. How Kangaroos Live

    A. Life cycle and living habits

        1. Live about fifteen years

        2. Some live in colonies, some live alone

        3. Some come out at night, others at day

        4. Like to sun bathe and bathe in river

    B. Eating habits

        1. _____

          _____

        2. Smaller kangaroos eat insects, roots, fruit, berries

    C. Offspring

        1. One baby at a time

        2. _____

        3. Called a "joey"

Complete this activity.

2.31 Fill in the details left out of the outline on kangaroos. Use the notes from the information on kangaroos.

You will now organize the notes you took on your Bible topic into an outline. Study your notes and decide on three or four main topics.

 Complete the following activity.

2.32 Write your topic and main topics on the blanks. If you only have three main topics, leave the fourth one blank.

_____

My topic

I. _____

II. _____

III. _____

IV. _____

Review your notes again and decide on subtopics and details that would fit under each topic. In outlining you may never have just one subtopic under a main topic. You must have at least two or more subtopics for each main topic.

Choose details from your notes. Remember details should be related to the subtopics, and the subtopics related to the main topics.

 Complete these activities.

2.33 On a separate piece of paper, complete your outline for a Bible topic. Rearrange and correct as needed.

2.34 On a separate piece of paper, copy your outline in your best handwriting. Have the outline checked by your teacher.

TEACHER CHECK _____ _____
initials   date

SPELLING AND HANDWRITING

In this section you will learn to spell more two-, three-, four-, and five- syllable words. You will also improve your skills in writing individual letters.

Spelling. When dividing a word into syllables, syllable patterns can help us know where to divide the word.

One common pattern is to divide words between consonants.

　　Example: Sen / tence

Some of your spelling words will follow this pattern.

You will learn to spell some three-syllable words where a single vowel in the middle is a syllable.

　　Example: med / i / cine

You will study four- and five-syllable words that end in the suffixes -ary, -ity, -tion, -ent, and -al.

Learn to spell the words from Spelling Words-2.

SPELLING WORDS-2

almost	eternity	organization
cafeteria	exaggeration	origin
chocolate	glorify	pardon
comment	international	public
Congress	medicine	senator
customary	necessity	superintendent
dictionary	ordinary	

 Copy the spelling words in your best handwriting.

2.35 Spelling Words-2

　　a. _____　　b. _____

　　c. _____　　d. _____

　　e. _____　　f. _____

　　g. _____　　h. _____

　　i. _____　　j. _____

　　k. _____　　l. _____

　　m. _____　　n. _____

　　o. _____　　p. _____

　　q. _____　　r. _____

　　s. _____　　t. _____

Complete the following activities. You may use a dictionary.

2.36 Write the five two-syllable words that have the syllables divided between two consonants.

Divide each word into syllables.

a. _____ b. _____

c. _____ d. _____

e. _____

2.37 Write the four three-syllable words with a single vowel syllable in the middle.

Divide each word into syllables.

a. _____ b. _____

c. _____ d. _____

2.38 Write the one three-syllable word that does not follow the preceding pattern.

Divide the word into syllables.

_____

2.39 Write the five four-syllable words with suffixes -*ary* and -*ity*. Divide each word into syllables.

a. _____ b. _____

c. _____ d. _____

e. _____

2.40 Write the four five-syllable words with suffixes -*tion, -ent,* and -*al*.

Divide each word into syllables.

a. _____ b. _____

c. _____ d. _____

2.41 Write the one five-syllable word with two single vowels as separate syllables.

Divide the word into syllables.

_____

Write the correct word(s) to complete each sentence.

2.42 The a. _____ announced to the b. _____ that he will introduce his

new bill when c. _____ meets.

2.43 The school a. _____ visited our b. _____ to try our new lunch
program.

2.44 The a. _____ one day hopes to be b. _____ and deliver Bibles all over the world.

2.45 It was a a. _____ to give the sick child the correct b. _____ immediately.

2.46 John's a. _____ about his twenty-five-inch trout was an b. _____ .

2.47 It is a. _____ to use the b. _____ to check the meanings of words.

2.48 The old woman's native a. _____ was Norway, and she was no b. _____ person, but a remarkable woman.

2.49 He a. _____ dropped his b. _____ candy when he slipped on the wet pavement.

Read the following verses in your Bible. Write one word from each verse that is a spelling word.

2.50 Isaiah 55:7 _____

2.51 Isaiah 57:15 _____

2.52 Psalm 22:23 _____

TEACHER CHECK _____ _____
                    initials   date

ABC **Ask your teacher to give you a practice spelling test of Spelling Words-2.** Restudy the words you missed.

Handwriting. The letters *c* and *e* can often be confused with other letters if they are not made properly. If the curve is not completed on the *c*, it can look like an *i*.

Correct

c

Incorrect

c

If the loop on the *e* is not open, it also can look like an *i*.

Correct

e

Incorrect

e

Find the *c*'s and *e*'s in the following poorly written words. Rewrite the words correctly.

2.53 a cold region   *arctic*   _____

calm   *peaceful*   _____

a fire-maker   *charcoal*   _____

a noise   *crackle*   _____

keeps track of days and months   *calendar*   _____

a force   *energy*   _____

think hard   *concentrate*   _____

occupation   *career*   _____

wear on your wrist   *bracelet*   _____

safe   *secure*   _____

TEACHER CHECK _____ _____
                        initials   date

Review the material in this section in preparation for the Self Test. This Self Test will check your understanding of this section as well as your knowledge of the previous section.

SELF TEST 2

Write true or false (each answer, 2 points).

2.01 _____ Proverbs are not poetry in the same way psalms are.

2.02 _____ The Hebrew proverbs belong to Christians as well as to the Hebrews.

2.03 _____ You should always use only one source for a report.

2.04 _____ Jesus often used parables in His teaching.

2.05 _____ Parables are never explained.

2.06 _____ Your topic choice will decide where you will go for your information.

2.07 _____ Hebrew poetry never rhymes.

2.08 _____ Prophetic writing is only found in books of the Bible known as The *Prophets*, or *prophetic writing*.

2.09 _____ When taking notes for a report, you should only write down the main ideas.

2.010 _____ Making two parts of a sentence or two sentences balance is called parallelism.

Write the letter of the correct match (each answer, 2 points).

2.011 _____ have few characters.

2.012 _____ are an example of Hebrew poetry.

2.013 _____ is a short teaching story.

2.014 _____ are a record of utterances by prophets.

2.015 _____ is a characteristic of Hebrew verse used in proverbs and psalms.

2.016 _____ is an example of poetic prose.

2.017 _____ should be specific.

2.018 _____ in the Old Testament was often meant to be sung.

2.019 _____ are short sayings that suggest good principles.

2.020 _____ helps you organize information for a report.

a. A parable

b. Proverbs

c. Short stories

d. A topic choice

e. Parallelism

f. Hebrew poetry

g. The Psalms

h. The Beatitudes

i. Prophetic writings

j. Details

k. Outlining

Complete the following statements (each answer, 3 points).

2.021 Short stories have _____ descriptions.

2.022 The Pentateuch consists of the first five books of the _____ Testament.

2.023 Short stories cover a _____ time period.

2.024 The topic, *The World*, would be too _____ .

2.025 Two Old Testament books written entirely in poetry are a. _____ and

b. _____ .

2.026 "As the sword of a mighty man," and "as the stones of a crown" are examples of

_____ .

2.027 All prophecy should be studied under the direction of the _____ .

2.028 Subtopics in an outline should be related to the _____ .

2.029 Notes are easily organized if they are written on _____ .

2.030 You should write questions you would like answered in a report and decide on the

_____ for writing the report before you take notes.

Write the letter of the correct answer on the line (each answer, 2 points).

2.031 A short story has action, setting, and _____ .
a. characters   b. a moral   c. parallelism

2.032 "The wise shall inherit glory: but shame shall be the promotion of fools" is an example of a

_____ .
a. poem   b. parable   c. proverb

2.033 "A soft answer turneth away wrath" is parallel to _____ .
a. "for out of it are the issues of life."
b. "but grievous words stir up anger."
c. "but the righteous are bold as a lion."

2.034 "The merciful man doeth good to his own soul" is parallel to _____ .
a. "but the forward tongue shall be cut out."
b. "but in the multitude of counselors there is safety."
c. "but he that is cruel troubleth his own flesh."

2.035 An example of a specific topic is _____ .
a. The Effect of Pollution on Fish
b. Science
c. People in the Bible

2.036 Psalm 119 is an example of _____ .

    a. acrostic   b. a parable   c. prophecy

2.037 John 3:16 is _____ .

    a. poetry   b. poetic prose   c. a parable

2.038 Three purposes for writing a report are to entertain, inform, and _____ .

    a. convince   b. complete an assignment   c. organize

2.039 The three main parts of an outline are main topics, subtopics, and _____ .

    a. subpoints   b. notes   c. details

2.040 Notes for a report should be _____ .

    a. written in complete sentences

    b. copied exactly as from the original

    c. written only as main ideas in your own words

Answer the following questions (each answer, 5 points).

2.041 What are two characteristics of Hebrew poetry?

_____

_____

_____

_____

_____

_____

_____

_____

2.042 What are two characteristics of Hebrew prophecy?

_____

_____

_____

_____

_____

_____

_____

_____

80/100	SCORE _____	TEACHER _____ _____
		initials date

ABC **Take your spelling test of Spelling Words-2.**

3. SECTION THREE

In Section 3 you will study the literary forms in which Bible history and Law are written. You will learn why Bible history is different from other history. You will learn the final steps of report writing and finish your own report. You will learn to spell some of the literary terms you have read in this LIFEPAC and practice writing the letters *h* and *z*.

Section Objectives

Review these objectives. When you have finished this section, you should be able to:

1. Identify seven Bible literary forms.
10. Tell why Bible history is different from other history.
11. Tell what is meant by the term "The Law" as used to identify Bible writing.
12. Draft, correct, and finalize a written report.
13. Spell new words correctly.
14. Correctly form letters.

Vocabulary

Study these words to enhance your learning success in this section.

codified (kōd′ u f īd). Arranged according to some system.

impose (im pōz′). Put a burden, tax, or punishment on.

incidental (in′ su den tul). Happening or likely to happen in connection with something else.

penalty (pen′ ul tē). Punishment.

ritual (rich′ u̇ ul). A form of system of rites or solemn ceremony.

Pronunciation Key: hat, āge, cãre, fär; let, ēqual, tėrm; it, īce; hot, ōpen, ôrder; oil; out; cup, pu̇t, rüle; child; long; thin; /ŦH/ for then; /zh/ for measure; /u/ or /ə/ represents /a/ in about, /e/ in taken, /i/ in pencil, /o/ in lemon, and /u/ in circus.

BIBLE HISTORY AND LAW

Every day you inquire about many things. Such inquiry is the basic way of learning. The word *history* comes from a Greek word meaning *to inquire into or about*. A shortened form of this word is *story*. History is the telling of what happened, to whom it happened, who were the heroes, who were the villains, and how it all ended. Someone has said that the Christian should regard history as "His story." To regard it this way means to realize that, even though God allows man to make decisions which may be good or bad, God is in overall control. His purposes will be fulfilled. Bible history makes this fact clear because God caused the prophets to interpret history. God's Law, history, and prophecy should all be studied together. God's grand designs may be seen in this way. You have learned how to look at the prophetic writings. In this section you will learn the various forms in which God's Law and Bible history were written and where to look for them.

History. The books of history in the Old Testament are Joshua, Judges, Ruth, 1 Samuel, 2 Samuel, 1 Kings, 2 Kings, 1 Chronicles, 2 Chronicles, Ezra, Nehemiah, and Esther. You should learn this list of historical books. Although the five books of Moses—Genesis, Exodus, Leviticus, Numbers, Deuteronomy—are classified as Law, each contains some historical writing. Genesis is really pure history. Many of the prophetical writings contain **incidental** pieces of history.

Historical material may be gleaned from almost all of the New Testament books. Matthew, Mark, Luke, and John recorded the life and words of Jesus which resulted in the formation of His church on earth. In *The Acts of the Apostles*, Luke recorded the spread of the church throughout the Roman Empire. The Acts of the Apostles most closely fits the classification, historical book.

Several literary forms may be seen in the historical writing in the Bible.

1) Genesis is mostly written as *biographies* of certain people who were the ancestors of the Israelites. Joshua, Judges, Ezra, and Nehemiah are somewhat biographical. Ruth and Esther are biographical, but contain important historical information about the Israelite nation. The first two of the major historical books, 1 Samuel and 2 Samuel, are mostly biographical, even though they are concerned with the kingdom of Israel. The biographical material in the prophetic writings is incidental to the message. The four Gospels are biographical. The Acts contains biographical material about the Apostles.

2) 1 Kings, 2 Kings, 1 Chronicles, and 2 Chronicles contain more straightforward *historical writing* than any of the others. Both pairs of books are heavily biographical about the early kings of Israel and Judah but record the acts of the later kings in a more routine way.

Write true or false.

3.1 _____ Genesis records the lives of people who were the ancestors of the Israelites.

3.2 _____ The word *history* comes from a Greek word meaning to inquire into or about.

3.3 _____ Ruth and Esther are stories; therefore they are fiction.

3.4 _____ No historical writing occurs in the prophetical books.

3.5 _____ The four Gospels are largely biographical.

3.6 _____ Many of the nonhistorical books contain incidental pieces of history.

3.7 _____ The major historical book of the New Testament is Acts.

Complete the following activity.

3.8 List the books that are classified as the historical books of the Old Testament.

a. _____   b. _____   c. _____

d. _____   e. _____   f. _____

g. _____   h. _____   i. _____

j. _____   k. _____   l. _____

Law. Although the five books of Moses are classified as the books of Law, the Law itself is found in Exodus chapter 19–40; in Leviticus; and in Deuteronomy 4:44–30:20.

The form in which the Law is written is called a _code_. A _code_ is a systematic collection of laws. Literary devices, figurative speech, and narrative have no place in a code. A code must be as exact and as clear as possible. Since **penalties** are **imposed** for breaking a law, the law must be easily understood. Not all laws of every country meet this standard, but the Mosaic Law did.

The laws were given to Moses by God. For this reason they are referred to as the Mosaic Law, just as the first five books of the Bible are referred to as the books of Moses.

The basic commandments are the Decalogue—The Ten Commandments—given in Exodus 20:1–17 and repeated in Deuteronomy 5:6–21. Strong warnings were given about the necessity of keeping these laws. God told the people of Israel (Deuteronomy 5:32), "...Ye shall not turn aside to the right hand or to the left."

In addition to the basic laws, a complete code of laws governing all parts of Hebrew life was given. This law was the _ceremonial law_. If any of these laws were broken by an Israelite, the code gave the exact offering and **ritual** that would

| Commandments

restore the person to fellowship with God and his fellow Israelite.

The chief characteristics, then, of the Mosaic Laws were that they were **codified** and written clearly. Every Christian should know the Ten Commandments, either in the language of the Bible or in the briefer form that is often taught in Sunday schools.

The New Testament records that Jesus said the Law of Moses was given by God and would be fulfilled by Him (Matthew 5:17–19). He kept the basic moral law. The elaborate ceremonial law, the laws of the offerings, were fulfilled in Christ's sacrifice of Himself on the Cross. These offerings of animals are no longer required. Christ asks of us instead spiritual offerings.

Read Exodus 20 and complete the verses.

3.9 I am the Lord _____

_____ .

3.10 Thou shalt have _____ .

3.11 Thou shalt not make unto thee _____

_____

_____ .

3.12 Thou shalt not bow down thyself to them, _____ : for I the Lord thy God am a jealous God, visiting the iniquity of the fathers upon the children unto the third and fourth generation of them that hate me;

3.13 And showing _____

_____ .

3.14 Thou shalt not take _____

for the Lord will not hold him guiltless that taketh his name in vain.

3.15 Remember the sabbath day _____ .

3.16 Six days shalt thou labor, _____ .

3.17 But the seventh day is _____ :
in it thou shalt not do any work, thou, nor thy son, nor thy daughter, thy manservant, nor thy maidservant, nor thy cattle, nor thy stranger that is within thy gates:

3.18 For in six days the Lord made the heaven and earth, the sea and all that in them is, and

rested the seventh day: wherefore _____

_____ .

3.19 Honour _____ that thy days may be long upon the land which the Lord thy God giveth thee.

3.20 Thou shalt not _____ .

3.21 Thou shalt not _____ .

3.22 Thou shalt not _____ .

3.23 Thou shalt not bear _____ .

3.24 Thou shalt not covet thy neighbor's house, thou shalt not covet thy neighbor's wife, nor his manservant, nor his maidservant, nor his ox, nor his ass, nor _____

_____ .

TEACHER CHECK _____ _____

initials   date

REPORT WRITING

If you have followed all the steps in getting ready to write a report, you will have little trouble actually writing the report.

In this section you will draft, correct, and finalize your report on a Bible topic.

| Check your draft. Does it need corrections?

Drafting. Drafting means to write a rough draft, or copy. You use the outline prepared from note cards. Remember this writing is a "rough" draft. Don't be too concerned with spelling and punctuation now. Instead try to make your ideas clear and flow from one paragraph to the next. Review the section on writing paragraphs in Language Arts LIFEPAC 605. New paragraphs often are made for each topic and occasionally for subtopics and details.

Correcting. After your rough draft is written, you go back over it and make corrections. Check spelling, punctuation, complete sentences, and clear ideas. Ask yourself how you can improve it.

Finalizing. After correcting the rough draft, the report is ready to be finalized, or finished. The title or the report is written at the top of the page. Remember to indent for each new paragraph. Number each page at the bottom if the report consists of more than one page.

Review the material on outlining in Section 2. Read again the outline of a report about kangaroos. This part has been written from the first main topic of the outline.

Example:

Kangaroos

When we talk about kangaroos, we usually think about the large kind we see in the zoo. However, kangaroos come in many different sizes. Wallaby is a name for a small kangaroo. The large animals are called kangaroos. The smallest kangaroo is only eighteen inches long. Some kangaroos are about the size of a rabbit. The largest kangaroo is about five to seven feet tall and weighs two hundred pounds.

Kangaroos have long, large hind feet and powerful tails. They use their tails to help balance themselves. Kangaroos are grey and brown in color.

Usually a shy and gentle creature, kangaroos can hop five to ten feet. When they are traveling fast, they can leap an amazing fifteen to twenty feet.

Complete the following activity.

3.25 Study the preceding section on kangaroos. Compare it to the outline. On a separate piece of paper, write a rough draft for the main topics "Where kangaroos live" and "How kangaroos live." Use the outline and the notes. Check over your rough draft for spelling, punctuation, complete sentences, and clear ideas. Rewrite your Bible topic rough draft on the lines below.

_____

_____

_____

_____

_____

_____

_____

_____

_____

_____

_____

_____

_____

_____

_____

_____

_____

_____

Complete this activity.

3.26 On a separate piece of paper, copy your final report on a Bible topic in your best handwriting.

TEACHER CHECK _____ _____
                                    initials   date

SPELLING AND HANDWRITING

In this section you will learn to spell literary words. In handwriting you will practice the letters *h* and *z*.

Spelling. As you read the new list of spelling words, you will soon recognize words used in this LIFEPAC or in other LIFEPACs you have studied in the past year.

Now you will learn how to spell some of the forms and terms of literature and Bible literature.

Learn to spell the words from Spelling Words-3.

SPELLING WORDS-3
---

acrostic	imagery	personification
Biblical	lament	prophecy
biographical	law	prophetic
descriptive	literary	proverb
drama	literature	repetition
historical	metaphor	simile
history	parable	

Copy the spelling words in your best handwriting.

3.27 Spelling Words-3

a. _____   b. _____

c. _____   d. _____

e. _____   f. _____

g. _____   h. _____

i. _____   j. _____

k. _____   l. _____

m. _____   n. _____

o. _____   p. _____

q. _____   r. _____

s. _____   t. _____

Complete the following activities.

3.28 Write the spelling words derived from the following words. Notice how the *y* changes to *i* in each new word. Circle the *i* in each new word.

a. biography   _____

b. history   _____

c. personify   _____

3.29 Write the spelling word derived from the following word. Notice how the final *e* changes to an *i*. Circle the *i*.

Bible   _____

3.30 Write the spelling word derived from the root word, *describe*. Notice how the *b* changes to a *p*. Circle the *p* in the new word.

describe   _____

3.31 Write the word literature, then write the spelling word derived from literature.

a. _____   b. _____

3.32 Write the four spelling words that have the letters *ph* which sound like *f*.

a. _____   b. _____

c. _____   d. _____

3.33 Find *imagery* in the dictionary. Write the word and its pronunciation. See how they differ.

a. _____   b. _____

3.34 Write the spelling word which has only one syllable. _____

3.35 Write the three spelling words with two syllables.

a. _____ b. _____ c. _____

3.36 Write the spelling word which ends in a long /ē/ sound. _____

3.37 Write the words *acrostic* and *parable*. Divide them into syllables.

a. _____ b. _____

3.38 Fill in each blank with the correct letter so the completed word matches its definition.

a. _____
b. _____
c. _____
d. _____
e. _____
f. _____
g. _____
h. _____
i. _____
j. _____

a. A short fictitious story with a moral or spiritual truth

b. Having to do with the Bible

c. Having to do with prophecy

d. A prophet's declaration of something to come

e. Life or character(s) portrayed in a composition of dialogue designed for a stage production

f. Commandment of will of God

g. Record of past events, people, and so forth

h. Writings belonging to a certain language or people

i. Having to do with the written history of a person's life

j. Giving an account of a scene, person, thing, and so forth

TEACHER CHECK _____ _____
initials   date

Handwriting. You will practice the letters *h* and *z*. If you write these letters carelessly they can be confused with other letters. Study the examples.

This   *Not This*

h   *h*

z   *z*

Complete the following handwriting activities.

3.39 Practice writing the letters *h* and *z*. Write a row of each letter.

_____

_____

_____

_____

Read each sentence. One word in each sentence does not belong. Rewrite the sentence as it should read.

3.40 The zoo fed park the zebras.

_____

Izzy, a lizard, hurried into pretty a hollow log.

_____

Hazel drew a crazy, lazy horse paper.

_____

ABC **Ask your teacher to give you a practice spelling test of Spelling Words-3.** Restudy the words you missed.

Before taking the last Self Test, you may want to do one or more of these self checks.

1. _____ Read the objectives. See if you can do them.
2. _____ Restudy the material related to any objectives that you cannot do.
3. _____ Use the **SQ3R** study procedure to review the material.
   a. **S**can the sections.
   b. **Q**uestion yourself.
   c. **R**ead to answer your questions.
   d. **R**ecite the answers to yourself.
   e. **R**eview areas you did not understand.
4. _____ Review all vocabulary, activities, and Self Tests, writing a correct answer for every wrong answer.

SELF TEST 3

Write true or false (each answer, 2 points).

3.01 _____ A broad topic makes a good report.

3.02 _____ Descriptions are brief in short stories.

3.03 _____ Short stories in the Bible are not true.

3.04 _____ Jesus often used parables in His teaching.

3.05 _____ Parallelism is a type of short story.

3.06 _____ Always take notes in complete sentences for a report.

3.07 _____ History can be found in the New Testament and the Old Testament.

3.08 _____ Some historical writing also contains biographies.

3.09 _____ No historical writing occurs in the prophetical books.

3.010 _____ The stories of Ruth and Esther are fiction.

Write the letter of the correct match (each answer, 2 points).

3.011 _____ have few characters

3.012 _____ is characteristic of Hebrew verse used in proverbs of poetry

3.013 _____ is the Ten Commandments

3.014 _____ are a record of utterances by prophets

3.015 _____ was written in a form called code

3.016 _____ are short sayings that suggest good principles

3.017 _____ is a rough copy

3.018 _____ in the Old Testament was often meant to be sung

3.019 _____ is the telling of what happened, to whom, and how it ended

3.020 _____ is a short teaching story

a. Hebrew poetry

b. Proverbs

c. Short stories

d. Prophetic writings

e. Parallelism

f. Parable

g. History

h. Outline

i. The Law

j. The Decalogue

k. A draft

Complete the following statements (each answer, 3 points).

3.021 Organize information for a report by _____ .

3.022 "...Holy men of _____ spake as they were moved by the Holy Ghost."

3.023 A short story has a _____ , action, and characters.

3.024 "The fear of man bringeth a snare: but whoso putteth his trust in the Lord shall be safe," is
an example of a _____ .

3.025 The three parts of an outline are the _____ , subtopics, and details.

3.026 You should decide on the _____ for writing a report before you take notes.

3.027 The word _____ comes from the Greek word meaning *to inquire into* or *about*.

3.028 The laws were given to Moses by _____ .

3.029 The _____ are found in Exodus 20:1–17.

3.030 "Remember the Sabbath day to keep it holy," is an example of a _____ .

Write the letter of the correct answer on the blank (each answer, 2 points).

3.031 The action in a short story centers around _____ .
a. the characters
b. the setting
c. one happening or possibly two or three closely related incidents

3.032 The Pentateuch consists of _____ .
a. the first five books of the Old Testament
b. books in the New Testament
c. the Acts of the Apostles

3.033 Hebrew poetry _____ .
a. is really prose   b. always rhymes   c. never rhymes

3.034 Proverbs _____ .
a. are long poems
b. have the characteristic of parallelism
c. are short stories

3.035 All prophecy should be studied under the direction of _____ .
a. a good teacher   b. the Holy Spirit   c. a good textbook

3.036 "Where no counsel is, the people fall" is parallel to _____ .
a. "but in the multitude of counselors there is safety."
b. "but honor shall uphold the humble in spirit."
c. "but he that keepeth the law, happy is he."

3.037 A code found in the Old Testament is the systematic collection of _____ .
a. parables   b. proverbs   c. laws

3.038   Ceremonial law was _____ .
    a. the same as the Ten Commandments
    b. a complete code of laws governing all parts of Hebrew life
    c. did not have to be followed

3.039   The four Gospels are largely _____ .
    a. biographical   b. short stories   c. prophecy

3.040   The major historical book of the New Testament is _____ .
    a. Romans   b. Revelations   c. Acts

Answer the following questions (each answer, 5 points).

3.041   What is meant by the term "The Law" and how was it written?

_____

_____

_____

_____

3.042   After you finish an outline for a report, what are the next three steps and how do you go about them?

_____

_____

_____

_____

_____

_____

_____

_____

_____

_____

$\dfrac{80}{100}$ **SCORE** _____   **TEACHER** _____ _____
                                                                  initials   date

ABC

Take your spelling test of Spelling Words-3.

Before taking the LIFEPAC Test, you may want to do one or more of these self checks.

1. _____ Read the objectives. See if you can do them.
2. _____ Restudy the material related to any objectives that you cannot do.
3. _____ Use the **SQ3R** study procedure to review the material.
4. _____ Review activities, Self Tests, and LIFEPAC vocabulary words.
5. _____ Restudy areas of weakness indicated by the last Self Test.
6. _____ Review all Spelling Words in this LIFEPAC.